Inventing Angels

Books by Gary Fincke

   Poetry

      The Double Negatives of the Living
      Plant Voices
      The Days of Uncertain Health

   Short Stories

      For Keepsies

Inventing Angels

Poems by

Gary Fincke

Zoland Books
Cambridge, Massachusetts

First Edition published in 1994 by
Zoland Books, Inc.
384 Huron Avenue
Cambridge, MA 02138

Copyright © 1994 by Gary Fincke

All rights reserved. No part of this book may be used or reproduced in any manner whatsoever without written permission, except in the case of brief quotations embodied in critical articles and reviews.

FIRST EDITION

Text and cover design by Edith Allard
Printed in the United States of America

This book is printed on acid-free paper.

Library of Congress Cataloging-in-Publication Data

Fincke, Gary.
    Inventing angels: poems / by Gary Fincke. — 1st ed.
      p.   cm.
    ISBN 0-944072-39-9
    I. Title.
    PS3556.I457158   1994
    811'.54—dc20   93-38224
                                                                  CIP

Contents

A Murder of Crows

A Murder of Crows	3
The Book of Numbers	5
The Wonder Children	7
The Butterfly Effect	9
What My Mother Could Have Thought	11
The Theories for Ball Lightning	12
Rounds	13
The Skill of the Sunlight's Good	15
Ishi	16
Waiting for the Names	17
Remedies	18
The Congestive Failure of Belief	20
The Simple Language Which Damns Us	22
Every Reachable Feather	24

The Habits of Eating

The Habits of Eating	27

Inventing Angels

Inventing Angels	35
Where the Bakery Was	37
Learning Cursive	39
From Memory	42
Watching the Tied Boy	43
How to Verify God	45
Height	47
Junior Blackface	49
My Tennis Pro Is Shot	50
The Smokehouse	51
Home Treatments	52
Throwing the Voice	53
Oxygen	55
Thanksgiving	57

The Developer's Landscape

The Developer's Landscape   61

The High IQ of Nostalgia

The High IQ of Nostalgia   69
Callback   71
Commandments   73
Nigger Island   75
Booths   77
Behind Glass   79
The A Capella Rehab   81
Working the Eighteen-Inch Seam   83
U-turn   84
The Hot Wings Wager   86
The Snowball Protest   87
The Thoreau Cane   88
The Asthma Revenge   90
In the Census Year   94
The Hollow Earth   96

Acknowledgments

Some of these poems have been previously published in *ACM, Beloit Poetry Journal, Boston Literary Review, Pig Iron, Caprice, Cimarron Review, The Devil's Millhopper, The Gettysburg Review, Green Mountains Review, Images, The Journal, Kansas Quarterly, Kestrel, The Laurel Review, The Literary Review, The Missouri Review, New Collage, Painted Bride Quarterly, Pennsylvania Review, Poet & Critic, Poetry, Poet Lore, Poetry Northwest, Southern Poetry Review, Tar River Poetry, USA Today, West Branch, Yarrow,* and *Zone 3*.

"Inventing Angels" was reprinted in *Harper's Magazine*. "Watching the Tied Boy" (in an earlier version) and "Oxygen" appeared in the chapbook *Breath*, 1984, State Street Press. "The Book of Numbers," "The Butterfly Effect," "The Congestive Failure of Belief," "Throwing the Voice" appeared in the chapbook *Handing The Self Back*, 1990, Green Tower Press. "The Theories for Ball Lightning," "What My Mother Could Have Thought," "The Skill of the Sunlight's Good," "Watching the Tied Boy," appeared in *The Public Talk of Death*, chapbook 1991, Two Herons Press.

A Murder of Crows

A Murder of Crows

Driving home, I see all of them
By the highway, pecking at
Whatever is splayed out and torn,
And none of them flutter up
Or hop deeper on the shoulder.
The houses start to thicken,
The one set back from the road owned
By a woman who has been
Moved upstate for care. At the light,
I turn slowly and hear nothing
Promising in the noise the brakes
Make, how they remind me they
Will eventually fail, but
The man who lives next door says
He has a book for me downstairs,
And I have to watch him limp
Toward the dark, thinking how little
I read. I could stammer that
Words are ineffective as skin,
But I follow him and see
His cellar ceiling-high with books.
"Seventy-thousand," he says,
Nodding at the fire-hazard piles
Of them. We smile together
Though the room is impassable,
And I know I will never
Open the volume he hands me,
Vanity Fair, his seventh
Garage-sale copy, and I could
Repeat, "A labor of mules,
A drift of hogs," tell him about
The collective nouns for things,
How names can amuse us and do
Nothing to change this evening,
Whether the weight of this novel
Impresses me or he will

Follow it with others, stacking
Them in my arms and never
Imagining I could drop them.

The Book of Numbers

> Using a standard typewriter, Marva Drew, from 1968
> to 1974, typed the numbers from 1 to 1,000,000 on
> 2,500 pages.
> from *The Best of the Worst*

Fat with ambition, this book,
Though you can see how its plot
Must progress regularly
As wills in the careful scripts
Of scriveners. In this tale,
Everything says conclusion.
Each symbol, each myth predicts
A sort of Rapture when life
Goes blank as an end page, all
Of the story well-planned as
An Earth-centered universe.
I want, tonight, to say I've
Started that book of numbers
So often I think it's mine.
At least to a thousand, where
I've stopped; or once, ten thousand,
A weekend with childhood flu,
My aunt hauling the pages
Downstairs to ponder. "You got
Every number right," she said,
Reporting like proofreaders.
Ten thousand and one, I thought,
Ten thousand and two, and went
Outside, after that fever,
To bounce a ball off the roof,
Off the wall, to simulate
One tense game in a season
Of one hundred fifty-four.
And in ten years, if one group
Of believers is correct,
The world will explode because

That year matches the number
Of weeks Jesus walked the world.
The next year, too, will shatter
Us, a famous psychic claims,
And then the year 2000
Will send millions of hopeful
Up the mountains to welcome
The universal blindness.
So we need someone to count,
Take on a second volume
To insure we don't know how
It all turns out. "Pass it on,
No returns," we say, schoolboys
Punching the arms beside us.
Or circled, Boy Scouts, around
A campfire: "Jack still burning,"
Puffing on a glowing stick,
Handing it off before it
Goes black. One million and one,
Marva, one million and two . . .

The Wonder Children

His parents posed beside him, the latest
Child prodigy, thirteen, is tonight's good news.
He's entering medical school, puberty,

And the reporter is pleased to predict,
To say many of us will be grateful
For the certainty of his surgeon's hands.

Doogie Howser, she tries, citing sitcom
As if it were history, counting on
Most of us to know her network's lineup,

Though she could mention a hundred children
Sure with scalpels, repeat Mozart, Mill,
And Henry Truman Safford. Or tell us

The Willy Sidis story, not optioned
To television, not yet—his entering
Harvard, eleven years old; his leaving

Learning behind, saying *no* to lectures
And libraries with a self-inflicted
Resignation. How he adopted the broom

And mop. How his hands welcomed the scythe,
Stacked the streetcar transfers he treasured.
How he died, forty-six, in a rented room,

Outliving a host of precocious children:
Cardiac, master of languages, dead
At seven; the Infant of Lübeck,

The Bible's index, expired at four, each
A wonder child forever. And another
Mapped the only route to the needle's-eye

Entrance to heaven. Calculated the miles.
Established the angle of ascension.
And left the precise point of departure

For some future child genius to figure:
Including the rate of change for all things,
Their positions within the shifting sky

To one thousandth of a second as we
Revolve and spin, as each location in
The universe simultaneously moves.

Like our moon, we know, which is spiraling
Away from earth, and, in a million years,
Will be too distant to eclipse the sun.

The Butterfly Effect

> If a butterfly flaps its wings in Brazil, it might produce a tornado in Texas.
>
> from *The Laws of Chaos*

Early in the newsmagazine
these Haitian women are wailing,
and those that are not are holding
their breath and the hands of men
tense with a bullet expectation.
And I've read, too, that the wind
tonight may have originated
from their mourning, the beating
of their arms in the air sending
this record warm front north.
I've read about fractals,
the Russian Dolls of the universe,
diamonds made of diamonds made
of diamonds diminishing in size;
I've learned the Butterfly Effect,
how chaos is not chaos,
how some slaughter in Haiti flaps
its wings and churns into my grip
on the arm of my son, my clenched teeth
and hiss as he flutters his free arm
and wails and changes the future
of weather in a country east of us
where a father will choose, he thinks,
to stun his son to obedience.
And when I leave him to let the dog
walk me into sense, the unnatural wind
chatters the branches that skitter her
to a barking panic on our street
of sculpted shrubbery where Christmas bulbs,
in one yard, might be arranged
into language if you're properly
angled, upstairs, across the street,

positioned like an antenna straining
for a distant station, my son in his window
watching me handle the dog, my breath
without its winter clouds, nothing he'd believe
could join the southern grief of a warm front.

What My Mother Could Have Thought

For a while, she was almost successful
Turning complaints into silence. She packed
Drawers of tools with wrenches, Phillips heads,
Catchalls for despair. There was a promise:
She opened a hymnal every Sunday
And the verses spoke directly to her.
Hosannah, she might have sung on her way
To repair; Holy, she might have whispered
To whatever she fixed. She understood
Tools, how to get things shipshape at least once
A day. There'd be a moment so quiet
She'd imagine everybody she loved
Had been saved, and standing in her kitchen,
The drawers all closed, she imagined us sewn
Into a quilt, huge patches of purple
And gold. All of our stories would cover
Her, and she would pull them under her chin
And listen to how those voices warmed her.

The Theories for Ball Lightning

Mr. Smink told us the history of the high-school band,
Which boys had fainted in parades, which girls had soloed
To applause. We smeared "Camptown Races," blatted
"Yankee Doodle"; Mr. Smink explained how our music
Traveled through space, how it would play forever
On a frequency someone green might hear. Lately,
He'd been spiraling from seniors to fourth-graders,
Repeating FACE and Every Good Boy Deserves Fudge
As if Martians might love mnemonics. After us
Were third-graders with rental horns, second-graders
With tonettes, but he picked us to tell how
His friend had been killed by music, his radio
Plunging into the tub when he reached for soap.

We understood nobody would die for the songs
We were practicing, but we wanted to fill
A bathtub, tip someone's Philco into the water
While "Sugartime" or "Tammy" was on the air,
Zapping one horror on the launchpad. We hoped
There'd be lightning, some Shazam bolt of weather
In the locked bathroom. We asked Mr. Smink
If the electrocuted glowed, and he told us
About the woman who claimed a cloud of light
Pursued her, how she brushed its lecher's touch
From her arm and it exploded. We finished
"Oh, Susanna." We blew our spit on the wooden floor
And listened to Mr. Smink recite the theories
For ball lightning: Bubbles of burning methane;
Swarms of glowing pollen; throngs of electrified gnats—
As if that woman had eaten badly before the attack,
Bringing a visit from an electronic Marley's ghost,
Something like seeing the luminous crews who piloted
Their saucers transfixed by our beginners' tunes.

Rounds

> Cancerous cells speed up their activities every 20 hours
> instead of the normal 24,
> from *The Body in Time*

Four cars fill my neighbor's slanted driveway.
He backs one to the street, parks, reverses
Another, parks and replaces the first
Before driving twenty miles out of town
To teach, for his living, the children
Of farmers to harmonize. I listen
To the morning's squabble apocalypse,
The recurring complaints from my trio
Of children, each of them slamming into
Separate rooms to raise the squeal or growl
Of a favorite song turned "Frère Jacques"
If I position myself correctly.
My neighbor, today, could be teaching rounds.
He could be introducing wake-up songs
Or lullabies to lessen the fear of sleep
Or the slick wig of chemotherapy
He's been lately wearing. Listen, he's said,
My students will soon lapse into spitballs
And chewing gum in the lock, but someone's
Discovered there are sound waves on the sun.
Each has a different frequency, zigzags
Through fire, plunges toward the core, and rebounds
To break the surface, making it swell
And shrink like a heartbeat. All the while,
Shivering with cyclical starquakes,
The sun rings, if we could hear, like a gong.
And I recalled the science whiz, in school,
Who changed the frequency of a classroom
Outlet, plugged in the clock, which ran faster,
Now, by ten percent. And the professor
Went faster as well, speaking more quickly
To cram in his lecture notes. What a joke,

We thought, when the student readjusted
The outlet, further hastening the time.
The teacher turned auctioneer; my neighbor
Should test the outlets in every room
He enters, searching for the strange cycle
Which refutes the sun. In Singapore,
In five months, eighteen young Thais, otherwise
Healthy, have died in their sleep. Which could mean
Lifestyle, job stress, congenital failures
Of the heart; but six hundred Thai workers,
All male, in the Middle East, have recently
Slept to death, and more that a hundred U.S.
Cases of such sudden death syndrome
Have been reported, sufficient, I'd say,
To warrant the Thai whisper of "lai tai,"
The nightmare death where widow ghosts spirit,
During sleep, young men away as husbands
Eternal. Now some of them, each night,
Paint their fingernails red, believing
Those phantoms might think them women and choose
Elsewhere, attributing nothing to
The circadian rhythms of their bodies:
The pain threshold which lowers at night,
The immune system which always weakens,
Our cells branded by the solar cycle
With "about a day." Such evidence we have:
How heliotropes open and close
Their leaves although the sun is absent.
How fruit flies take to flight before noon,
Generation after generation,
Even the dimly lit, first soaring at ten.
And the improbable cycles of joy,
Our next unfurling in the dark despite
The unlikely return of the light.

The Skill of the Sunlight's Good

The miracle animals approach, creep
Forward like the Ugandan Tortoise,
Who talked from his shell, or leap
Like Chris, the Psychic Dog, barking
Futures. They nod, paw, tap hooves—
And Lady Wonder, the Telepathic Horse,
Put her nose on oversize keys to print
Fortunes. What typos to hunt and peck;
She nudged and pressed, prophecy if you
Bought "The Skull of the Sinlight's Goof."
She could have been an economist,
Could have run for office and dictated
Letters to secretaries hired to follow
The mute inflections of her grammar.

Which of us scoffs? We won't harm anyone
With an ESP for heaven, mouthing hymns,
Chanting phrases of faith. There were weeks
I memorized Bible verses, recited them
At the altar, and I wasn't crippled.
This week I've sung "The Old Rugged Cross"
And repeated the standard prayer
Of the church aloud. And in public.
After I said "Amen," a child I'd known
Was off to burial. So be it.
So the animals use four legs forward
And do wonderful things if we let
Our mouths open to the old words of snort
And bark and nicker, saying, "Of course."

Ishi

> In 1911, a Yahi Indian, previously thought extinct,
> reappeared, and remained well known until his death.

You've come to see the last Yahi Indian,
The one who's turned up though his tribe's extinct,
Something like a dodo on the doorstep,
Somebody who needs a name though he can't
Repeat it. Taboo, he says, and why not,
Our names as powerless as fish-bone oaths.
Try *Ishi*. Try the word in your language
For *man* and let the leveler in it
Keep you quiet. That last Yahi carries
Enough obsessive words. Listen to him
Repeat "Deer Creek Canyon Slaughter," naming
The method for making the Yahi scarce,
This *Ishi* famous, forty years later,
For being alive, such celebrity
You might record his oral recipe:
Take all of one kind, bunch them together
And kill them. Leave twelve to live but make sure
They never touch. Now wait until there's one.
Pay attention for five years. He'll die, too.
Ishi. You are not allowed to say it.

Waiting for the Names

In this wet autumn my father brings
His gift of shrubbery. He digs
After dinner along the borders
Of my lot, lifting the heavy soil
Like the slush of an early snow.
His transplants, he believes, will
Survive like hearts if I am careful.
"None of these need be lost," he says,
When I join him as I must, waiting
For the names, their spring colors,
But he doesn't speak again
To my backyard obedience,
The burden, at forty, of being son,
Indifferent to which of these leaves
Will be lost. Whatever is going wrong,
This evening, has six months to be
Secret, a schoolgirl's pregnancy,
The final loose-bloused weeks
When query turns to sneer, blame
Fixed and permanent. The rumor
Of who we are is overdubbed
On the rippled dark like echoes
Of our voices, impersonal, nomadic,
Drifting here to there, here to there,
Finally quiet or unheard.

Remedies

Yesterday, in court, the killer
Claimed he was a holy assassin
Because God had asked him to murder.
"I am a remedy," he said
Like a junta, and Shannon rides
With me to his shooting street,
Stuck in a flagman's traffic
This morning beside a mile-long
Graveyard for cars. She guesses
Half a million rust bodies
Are taking the cure, enough,
Maybe, to be Guinness famous,
And I answer by wheezing
Like an ad opener for
The inhalants I refuse.
It's stress, the road crew slouching
On shovels while I remember
The list-book lines on Salisbury,
The man who became a food when
He convinced his patients to eat,
Well done, ground beef three times
A day. "With hot water," he added,
Menu for the end of asthma.
"With reasonable habits."

Lately, I've been unreasonable,
Weaning myself from a thousand
Milligrams per day of Theolair
And waking inside the mathematics
Of strangling. So far, I've survived,
Walking breath back into myself,
Researching holistic remedies
For health: In Ethiopia,
For instance, one emperor
Ate the Bible to restore himself—
Psalms for discomfort, Exodus

For disease. He sent Zechariah,
Not hamburger, to his bronchi;
He swallowed Genesis instead
Of apricot pits or brain waves,
Choosing from his personal list
Of *lubberwort*, one word I've taught
Shannon, explaining her diet,
The valueless foods that make us
Stupid: her soda and puffed cheese,
The beer that squats on my lungs.
She's been sick enough to pry
Prescription tubes; she's recovered,
Returned to *lubberwort*, and we
Finally escape construction,
Enter the killer's neighborhood,
The six-hundred block of mayhem
Where we park and half recall
The shape of the death-house tree
Behind the TV newsman, Shannon
Standing in front of four likely
Trunks until I catch the curve
Of a branch, the black fork jutting
Exactly the way God's gunman
Must have seen it before slipping
Inside, and she poses there, fist
To her mouth like a microphone,
Ready to speak to the air.

The Congestive Failure of Belief

For the first minute, it's a nightmare
House-loose, someone finally solving
The locked doors, someone dissatisfied
With the stereo and silverware
And drifting down the hall for bodies.

After midnight, in my own unease
With sleep, I'd been brooding down a list
Of reunion ills: the permanent
Ink of age, how watered values freeze
On the crust of my winter visit.

I'd had an hour, like always, to think
Behind the double dark of closed eyes;
I'd listened to my father below
In his basement reluctant to sink
Into the end of this holiday.

He'd spent all his meal talk on death, cash
Saved by sudden's undemanding care.
Insurance, he'd said, stocks, deeds, a will,
Nothing he'd mentioned before, a wash
Of worry in the familiar wine.

Below freezing, the barometer
Bleating snow-to-come, I need to drive
East before the weather enters town,
And now the new noise outside the door,
Not my father, who never rises

At night, not the familiar terror
Of stealth that demands light and voices.
In the dark, my breathing, my mother's,
Her doubled pace of mine a mirror
For the rhythms that will slow us all.

She is standing in the black of pause
As if I've choked and gone blue-quiet
In the cowboy's room across from hers,

And I listen in return because
I might measure the scars on her heart,

The congestive failure of belief.
She drops forty years in her stillness,
Sentry for crib death, come to lift me
To the reflexive noun for relief,
Clutched to her flow and gone to feeding.

The Simple Language Which Damns Us

The last night at my father's
We wrestled blue mildewed chairs
And a burst hot water tank
Up his cellar stairs. I listened
For the whistling hint of wheeze,
Watched for his heart's first stutter,
And tumbled into bed to dream
Him dead. Outside, a man shouted
Christ and *hell,* commas among
Complaints about dust and trash.
A woman answered from behind
A door, and I recognized
The Frys, neighbors who had lived
There forty years, who had nine
Children, one per year, trusting,
For a decade, the Catholic math,
Adding and adding to the sum
Of believers. He'd grown fat
Enough to ride like a golfer;
She was a relief map of veins;
And he shifted, finally,
To *shit* and *fuck* to punctuate
The parallel structure of hate.
I knew he hadn't worked or walked
A flight of stairs for ten years,
But I wished his bullhorn voice
Would burst, imagined it drained
Across his porch, mute veneer, and
Later, when I stirred to sirens
Launched from every right-angle point
Of the compass, plus, I swore,
From Pittsburgh, I stiffened, sure
Of the long-promised air raid
I'd forgotten the code for.
Two short, one long, I decided,
Sitting up to measure and

Listening hard for Jim Fry
To be cursing careless cleaning
Because nothing nuclear
Was pouring from the midnight sky.
Perhaps he'd agreed to peace,
But at last, child-foolish, I stood
To stare at the city, ten miles
Away, where the mushroom would form
While I vanished. The skyline seemed
A runway, all of its lights
A huge wash of future until
Sense brush-stroked pretargeted,
Unmanned missiles. Firestorm, fallout,
Failure of the heart, I mouthed,
Alternate blasphemies from
The simple language which damns us.
The hound of obscenity
Snuffled on my father's lawn,
Circled and squatted to mark
An edge to one more surveyed yard
With the selective scent of waste.
And I thought, let the Frys hear
Its panting by their Cyclone fence.
Let them listen closely to
Its pale, staccato breathing,
While every dog along the street
Suddenly harmonized with
Each long, scatological wail,
The one that says what it means
To do just before it kills us.

Every Reachable Feather

On Sundays, now, my youngest son completes
His confirmation schooling, has me check
The answers for his Bible-study homework:

Besides Jesus, who rose from the dead?
He's written Lazarus like the workbook
Wants, but I suggest figurative Jonah,

The fortunate falls of Adam and Eve,
Confusing my son and recalling
How a neighbor, dead this week, hated

His wife's parrot for its squawking echo.
Look at my snake, he'd say. Never a noise.
Hardly a mess. And he set that boa

Loose to coil around the parrot's cage.
That quiets it, he'd say, and finally
The parrot went mute, his wife complaining

It was crazy, that parrots who utter
Nothing are depressed, and I agreed
Because every reachable feather

Was gone. If it had hands, she told me,
It would have plucked its head, and I said,
"It looks like food," just before my neighbor

Wrapped his fat arms around the cage, pressed
His face to the bars as if he didn't
Fear for his eyes. There was madness,

The constrictor coiling as it must,
The parrot suffocating in the dark,
Reviving, reviving again,

A home-bound record for resurrection,
Plucked and crazed and skittering back to
The vacant eternity of owners.

The Habits of Eating

The Habits of Eating

The Ignition Point of Paper

The first evening of war, an hour
After firemen snatched our dinner
From the oven to fling it outside,
We watched a map of the Middle East
As if it were animated,
Those newsmen doing voice-overs
From countries so sure to suffer
The black blast of cartoon mayhem.

We listened to air raid sirens.
We heard *warhead, payload, range,* and
Wondered how much those reporters,
Self-consciously slow with gas masks,
Would sweat and twitch. And we started
Rethinking dinner, what else to eat
With war because "Chicken-in-a-Sack"
Lay charred and sprawled in our front yard.

I'd opened and closed the oven door.
I'd watched the cyanotic smolder
Through the glass, suddenly saying,
"Four fifty-one," remembering,
From school, a novel about books burned
By firemen, the classics flaring
Forty-nine degrees below the heat
Our recipe had set up for baking.

I'd felt like a science text, like
Bagging my own bookish body
For the torch. On television
The President stared and told us,
"This is no Vietnam," sounding
Like the President who told us,
"We'll nail the coonskin to the wall"
The year I learned the ignition point

Of paper. And I left the gospels
Of the President to resack that
Sorry chicken, add it to our week's
Curbside bags. Though, by daylight, something
Had shredded its way inside, scattered
The carcass on the snow, none of it
Retrieved by the garbageman
Who refuses what's not bagged and tied.

Inedia

Fire flares beneath a nearby village. Slime, a state away, bubbles up through stricken lawns. A week after war stories thin, two ruins return like soldiers. Here are the families shuttled from Love Canal calling their children in from fresh sludge; here are the relocated residents of Centralia learning the coal seams are burning their way to the colony. The sequel parents repeat their stalled health, the particular plights of their children. They talk about the hammerlock of property, the eyegouge of ownership. In one parable of industry are the blasphemies of coal barons; in the other are the heresies of the landfill. Such a sampler of sadness, we press our channels like chocolates, using our fingers to find cherries, butter creams, sweet stories of someone saved like the woman, just found, who lived two weeks without eating, the miracle explained by an expert who tells us she crash-dieted before her voyage to shipwreck. She'd grown used to little food, a sort of cross-training for starvation, and I recall the Woman of Norwich, who lived for twenty years without eating, according to Francis Bacon, who might be Shakespeare, according to someone else.

The Maggot Farmer

Lately, maggots swarm in our garbage
When the bags are carried to the curb.
I make lifting my son's job, tell him
They're only larvae, that we could use
Them for bait to hook barble and bream.
I mention the farmer who showed me
The carcasses of cattle he stored
Behind his house. "For coarse fishermen,"

He explained, while I stared, retreated,
And remembered Aristotle claimed
Maggots were conceived by rotten meat,
What we eat the presexual mother
Of flies. He thought he saw insects birthed
By mud; he wrote it down and landed
On a list of fools, one notch below
Bill Pickering, the astronomer
Who said, in this century, the spots
On the moon are huge swarms of insects.
Maybe he let his garbage grow wings
Instead of flushing his cans with spray.
Maybe NASA filmed the astronauts
In Nevada like the skeptics claimed
Because they feared the lunar surface
Writhed with grubs. And though my son insists
No one grows maggots for a living,
We've dropped worms into fouled creeks for sport
Or something to do. We've examined
The teeth we've found while digging for bait,
Thinking, if we studied forensics,
We might claim discoveries others
Would believe for as long as it takes
To turn up something to disprove them.

Don't Let the Moon Break Your Heart

At three a.m., in this B-movie,
An early Sixties dubbed-in saga
About Spaniards reaching the New World,
The Cortés look-alike steps ashore
Saying, "That's one small step for man."

So he might, in first run, have moved
Neil Armstrong to tears. Or all along,
Those astronauts, sworn to secrecy
In Nevada, were prepped for bogus
Landings with lines penned for beefcake stars.

David Scott. James Irwin. John Young.
I need an almanac, now, to name

The moonwalkers, sleeplessness enough
To discover crib-sheet dialogue
In old Conquistador films.

Early at work, the first year I taught
English to millworkers' children,
I let the night-shift guard say the moon
Just conquered lay fifty miles outside
Las Vegas, that close, as he showed me

A book which proved the earth flat, pointed
Out stars which clustered where heaven lay.
He explained the hierarchy of
Halo shapes, the maintenance for wings.
Some nights, he said, you can see shipments

Of the saved arriving in light—
The Pearly Gates, could I see their shape?
And I stared, two hours before I had
To say a word, mouthing to myself
"Don't Let the Stars Get in Your Eyes,"

Singing like an armored extra in
A foreign musical who's lip-synched,
Later, to show his hands flew apart
For balance, not joy, before he tumbled off
The delicate wafer of that just-claimed land.

The Mayan Syndrome

And now parts of our planet
Are missing. Soil presumed drowned.
Ozone kidnapped and murdered.
Such a pandemic, worldwide,
The rise of the Mayan Syndrome,

Even the ruins abused,
The man in this photograph
Sweeping his patio built
From temple blocks, feeding his pigs
From an artifact altar.

Nothing prospers, the man claims.
Rain's moved elsewhere, the solution
Of sea-turtle sacrifice
To the rain-god Chac proved false.
These swine need to eat, he says,

And I could smirk and imagine
That when their trough catches the sun
At the proper angle, the pigs
Pause to think of miracles;
But this week I've planted stones

Of my own, spreading them from
My sliding door in an $\sqrt{}$,
What might pass for a symbol,
The spread stones meant to be read
From the heavens to keep evil

From my doorstep, pass it on
To my neighbors—their daughter
Disappeared and likely dead—
Who aren't, in this drought month,
Pleading for rain when they face

Their altar. She won't be dead,
Not to us, they say, until
Her body's found. Like MIA's.
Like the charity bracelet names.
Corporal Connors, I read from

This one in my basement drawer,
And he's still missing somewhere
In a rain forest, immortal
Almost, like the souls of Mayans,
Like ozone and soil and

The woman who may be buried
In our neighborhood like one
Of those bodies cleverly
Hidden in the eye-teasers
Printed in a book of puzzles.

The Habits of Eating

Rabies. Bubonic plague. Now AIDS.
And *kuru,* the laughing sickness,
Hilarity easy to dodge.
This sure death comes from eating
The raw brains of the dead, gulping,
For prowess, defeated warriors.
So stupid, we scoff, so vain, yet
Stubborn we are, fierce with ethnic
Excuses for the animals
We devour: snake, dog, beetles, ants.
Or *Balot,* the Tagalog name
For one more long-lived recipe:
First, be patient. Wait the number
Of days it takes to hatch a duck,
And then snatch that egg, hard-boil
That fetus, eat the unborn whole.
Feathers, bill, and bones—you swallow
That unstroked duck down, estimate
The cost of lining the tract-length
Of yourself. "Like veal," you might say,
"Or lamb," like an illustrator
Of books for babies who want smiles
In their barnyards, ear-to-ear grins
On Flopsy, Mopsy, and Topsy.
And probably you've owned a few
Of those toys, and each one has died
Like a series of hamsters who
Quiver with metabolism
So rapid they flare and die like
Filaments. So we float and grow,
Transform from the curled worm common
To us all: Flippers to feet, tails
Retracted, the brain's circuitry
Connected, and, if not boiled,
Set loose by those who could eat us.

Inventing Angels

Inventing Angels

1

Let us explain, the church said, the mystery
Of the inexplicable bones. One: God ran tests,
What did we think? There's always waste—to get
Eden right, He had to fail a thousand times,
All those bones the rejected prototypes
For paradise. Two: God, for personal
Reasons, don't ask, created fossils. Wouldn't
You use omniscience for deceit? Wouldn't
You test your people with the illusion
Of previous life? Three: There were species
Too late for the ark, the animals at fault,
Indifferent to "All aboard." A pair
Of mammoths dawdled; the pterodactyls waffled;
Noah had enough to do with rationing,
With teaching the Peaceable Kingdom precepts.

2

Or Noah, we guessed, sensed that ark too small.
Afraid to blame God for the stupid specs,
He discreetly left half the world behind.
On Sundays, we learned the revised standard
Version of his story from a flannel board.
We followed felt cutouts through Noah's journey;
We heard reports on each Ararat attempt,
The church or celebrities funding those climbs
For the ark's splinters on the favorite
Mountain of the faithful. And we imagined
That cloth reshaped to everything preserved
By lava or tar whenever our teacher
Fast-forwarded to old Abraham and
The near-sacrifice he made following
The next audible orders from God.

3

The aurochs, quagga, great auk, and moa —
In the heresy of the backward glance,
An astonishment of passenger pigeons
Blackens the sky. One bird, its eyes sewn shut,
Is tied by hunters to a stool. And it calls
Loudly, of course, from the dark, drawing the flock
To the pogrom until nothing remains
But gangsters' slang, how we've used the dodo,
Which posed for artists, stood still for butchers,
The intent of predators bred from its genes.
What lasts? What lasts? A hundred years after
It disappeared, the flightless dodo turned
To hoax: Because there were no skeletons.
Because portrait art was weak evidence
Against the circumstantial disbelief.

4

The immediate doubt of the witness —
In each museum we read to verify
The bones, even those with hides or feathers
Like Martha, the last passenger pigeon,
Who was caged in the Cincinnati Zoo,
Who died and was not buried and rose again
As exhibit a year after Moreschi,
The last *castrato,* retired. The labels
On each of his ten recordings call him
The Soprano of the Sistine Chapel,
The church confessing to the altered truth
Of its soloists, inventing angels
We can visualize by listening
To the museum's gramophone, rapt with hearing
The pure, unnatural voice of extinction.

Where the Bakery Was

Last time my father
told me the story
of the drunk who knocked
on air and plunged right
through the lost doorway,
as surprised, falling,
as my father who
walks nightly into
the lot, pretending
his ovens still shove
bread upward. He named
the weeds; he opened
the thirty-year route
that I understand
because I stop here
with my children and
begin by saying
at seven o'clock
the bakery was lit
by the raw-wired road
into the freezer.
I was six years old
and stood in the smoke
smell of the morning
while my father paced
and shook things, testing
his will, and ten years
later I worked nights
for him, greasing pans,
arguing about
each girl I wanted
to prove myself with.
He said he dreamed that
his legs were sound, that
the borough had not
died under the last
settled Armco soot;

I told him nothing
about going for
their breasts, how they cried
out and I believed
this time I was not
mistaken. The dough
ran over the night;
the bars emptied at
two and my father
unlocked the door so
each desperate tongue
could finish something.
Which was what I heard:
how beer did little
for it, how stories
let their weight build up
until nothing could
reduce them. I knew
what they meant, frozen
sometimes by despair.
If someone would walk
back into that store
and buy those sweet rolls,
each one filled with cake
left-over and crushed
and moistened again
into something desired,
then it might not end
in the vacant lot
of progress, it might
not be the last time
I show my children
how work disappears,
say how some men, for
as long as they last,
return and retie
any uniform
that allows them to
walk into labor.

Learning Cursive

1

In second grade it was time to master
Cursive, starting with ovals repeated
Across the page. Around, around, around,
The teacher chanted, and we all managed.
We earned our inkwells; we jammed the steel points
Into place and held pens ready to write:
Dip, swirl, and don't rest the tip on paper.
We had blotters from the bank, last month stamped
On each; we had the Peterson Method
To learn unless we wanted to be fools
Like the inkwell spillers, the stained ones who
Were doomed to be goosequill failures, going
On relief, heading straight for the North Side
Soup kitchens we passed during a field trip.
And I started each exercise over
Until it was spotless like the confessed
Blank-sheet of myself, certain I'd succeed
If I could raise my hand enough, so much
A nonswimmer I felt fear of drowning.

2

This morning, the dog barks in the predawn dark at the window, and I lie deaf to what roused it until I hear a car door which could be neighbor, vandal, police, a son or daughter come home at 4:06 turning to 4:07 while I squint at the numbers as if they were the rough draft from a failed evening. And so frantic the dog becomes, I know my children aren't slinking across the lawn; and so long the held-breath half minute, I fear a knock, I bring a ringing to my ears.

Finally, nothing at the door. I'm safe from tragedy; the dog settles from its yapping so much like repeating the old ovals from school it might be tearing the tablet for its barks, going over and over the same lines as if it knows there's a next step through sound. And when it quiets, whoever was outside lost, I'm thinking cursive again, my penmanship swinging through the yammering of my

dog, its fear, mine, the silence of my wife's sleeping on her back
like the dead. I might as well be cave- bound. I have so little
defense the dog could tear my throat out if it mistook me, in the
dark, for one of the reasons it can't explain.

3

I was complaining about oxygen.
I was explaining to a colleague
How my office wouldn't light
If I meant to torch it, and she
Told me how she'd worked through
Three pregnancies in our building's
Poor air, how it accounted for
The flaws in her children, a sort
Of thalidomide from the workplace.

The consequences of breath:
She wrote her name; she scrawled,
To show me what her daughter
Had done, an autograph that ended
"Daltem" instead of the "Dalton"
She was. "She's learning cursive,"
She said, "and frightening us
With the alphabet," and I didn't
Think it odd at all that her
Daughter had changed her name
As if some blink in the genes
Had turned wide-eyed from prenatal
Air or a wish or despair.

4

Say you are seven again, stuck
In penmanship class, and this
Is the day you sign your name
To a paper, and then, astonished
By your signature, repeat yourself
Down the page as if you were
Every chapter in a novel.

You rush your table of contents
Home to your parents, unfold
That preface to your life,
And you think there's nothing
You're unwilling to write.
And this is the day you read
How many moments from now
Missiles will fly toward
The cities where your children
Will live, the day you decipher
The lists in cursive of toxic
Threats for their children, who
They'll resemble, what they'll
Write in cursive and carry home.
If that alphabet will be enough.
If their names will be legible
Or disconnected, perhaps, from
The evolution of ovals,
Webbed strangely like fingers
That mispronounce ourselves.

From Memory

One Sunday I recited the Bible's sixty-six books.
Both testaments. All the pronunciations
From Habakkuk to Ephesians to everything
I was willing to learn. I worked through a Psalm
A week, and nobody complained who had to listen.
My grade school friends didn't mind. They weren't
Wasting their time trying to match verses
With the minister's chosen one, and I
Total-recalled Genesis, Chapters 1 and 2,
Carried the creation to the pulpit. I was
Descending from heaven; I was apprentice
To salvation, and I memorized until the sky
Became a scroll that unrolled before my eyes
Like another miracle I doubted when I learned
There were alternate myths for this world.
The alphabet of absolutes drifted downwind
Like a morning's cirrus skyscape. The church
Stuffed itself with millhunks and their bloated wives,
And I was the son of nobody but a pair of people
Who sold bread and cakes to this congregation
Descended from the fisted thunderheads of lust.
Hymns, litanies, sermons — the church windows
Thrummed with passing trucks; the town's brutal clamor
Climbed the chancel while the words left me
Like my parents fleeing Eden. Suddenly, I lip-synched
For the blue signature of the Shakers,
For the audible mural of the streets,
For the raffle equation of worship
While another careless coal barge foundered
In the river behind that church, the language
Of its failure waiting for an elegy of explication.

Watching the Tied Boy

Indian fashion, we thought it was, to tie
Tommy Shereba to a white-barked tree
In the state preserve, and why we left him
Was his silence. None of us expected
A stoic who wouldn't confess or cry;
Nobody said, "How long?" while we hiked to
The service road. We were busy keeping
Branches from our eyes. There were jagged leaves
That opened our legs, a point we reached when
Tommy Shereba screamed like no actor
We'd heard, tangling us where the path
Confused itself for a knotted moment.
Whatever we felt, I slipped back to watch.
I crouched until numbness edged up my legs;
I stood and expected the leaves to drop
Like a dancer's fan. During those minutes
Of staring, I heard myself swallow, thought
The flesh would rot from both of us before
The resolution of stupid bondage.

That night, alone at ten-thirty, I watched
The story of a scientist turned mute
By torture. No one could help. They thought he'd
Been driven to madness by noise. I knew
The heartless on this show were Communists,
That the deaf and dumb victim, a free world
Hero, hadn't cracked. At last, one doctor
Solved the case, decided total silence
Made men lunatics for sound. He mentioned
Crickets, raindrops, the distant swish of cars.
He said the quietest place you know has
A comfort of sounds. And after they'd shocked
The patient back to sense, overloaded
Him with decibels, I sat in my room,
My parents an hour away, and heard all
The banalities of midnight, the creaks

And groans of stealth. I went to the window
Like the soon-to-be-murdered, looking for
The blade of the crazed, and saw that rescue
Relied on a vacuum, even the mites
Of sound sucked up, driven to some landfill
For bedlam where warnings were barbed enough
To keep us from the roared harm to hearing.

How to Verify God

By weighing the soul, putting the dying
On the sensitive scale we need
For balance: Someone, in 1907, did this,
A doctor who had access to death,
Those who could not refuse, and he
Measured one less ounce in those corpses,
Imagining flight as the beam dropped.

Well, I was glad to read about McDougall,
How faith, for once, can be shored up
By science, though there were plenty of hoots,
The kind I heard for being a Boy Scout,
An acolyte, a safety patrol captain,
All of them requiring a uniform
That made every thug in Pittsburgh jeer.

Over and over I had to walk Route 8
Where the trailer court made boys
Wear studs, where Pine Creek flooded
Each spring until nothing but poverty
Was left. I wanted a gun; I wanted
To watch all those sneering obscenities
Tumble back into the sewer of that creek —
What dark hands would instruct me;
What teacher, always a woman, would replace
My bandages with the silk touch of desire?

My cousin died. I lugged him
By one chrome handle and would not admit
The ache in my arm. My uncle died
And I staggered with that stranger,
Taking one sixth of him across Sharp's Hill,
Which will never be flooded, and that day
I could see how the mill's soot lay lower
Than us, caught in the valley by inversion.

That was my last pall-bearing. Our family's
Heavy Pittsburgh breath held while

I outgrew that duty, but I read later
That McDougall tested dogs, control group
For the soul, that he thought conversions
Would follow. Waiting was the hardest part,
Wishing for weight loss. There were times
When McDougall watched the chest of each man,
Sure this magic flew from the heart.
There was a blur, he thought, when the body
Lightened; the dogs, of course, lost
Nothing, the air around their dying still.

Height

In the played-out strip mine,
Left over from a soft coal decade
Before I was born, my father
Led us up a trail that
Peaked along the narrow crest
Of whatever was worthless,
And I finally had to kneel
And grip the ground with my hands,
Certain I was falling
Into the acid pool below.

If I want to show how peer pressure
Fails, I tell this story
And add how every boy who watched me
Whimper said nothing, how
My humiliated father
Had to lead me down like a suicide,
Taking the lengthy low route
Through the scrub trees until
We met the troop where the scars ended.

Well, it was like those first minutes
After anesthetic, checking down
The body for all the important parts,
But I've walked that path lately,
The land permanent scrap,
And the trail on the lip of the world
Is less frightening than a house roof,
My sons running along it
Without permission. And I thought
Of the precautions I have taken
With height, each unbalanced step
Backward when space leaps
In front of me, as obvious as Jack,
My roommate, who feared cancer
And insisted each mole was infected,
Testing himself with mirrors

In a self-destructive way.
And he was right, or at least
Heredity is chasing him, his mother
Cut and sewn, his father folded back
Together and dead within a month.

Look, I see the sense of it, bludgeoning
The self until it retreats from the edge.
Those that won't confess are listening
To their blood or testing their optic nerves
For wear. And walking back toward
The coward on the path, my father,
Who could not swim, might have been
Deep breathing, preparing himself for
That underwater time that lay beneath us.

Junior Blackface

"You look just like a little Al Jolson,"
My father said, and he asked me to try

"My Mammy," get down on one knee to plead
Theatrically for the past. My mother

Said "Stepin' Fetchit," though she was always
Insisting my shuffling, no-good, lazy

Habits were mirrors up to Hollywood.
I didn't mind playing Junior Blackface.

It would all wash off after I'd acted
The fool, part of "Amos 'n Andy Time,"

One year's Advent fund-raiser for the church.
Those big lips gave me happy feet, sure 'nuff,

One of my laughter lines, and you can fill
In the rest, recalling every stupid

Pickaninny soundtrack from your happy
Childhood. It's how we perform for adults.

Authority. The minister's wife wrote
The script. She sewed costumes and did makeup

And beamed when flashbulbs flared throughout her hit.
There were four weeks until Christmas; there were

Blessings, from her husband, on all of our
Upturned heads. So we waited, while he sang

In his Sunday School voice: Red and Yellow,
Black and White, they are precious in his sight;
Jesus loves the little children of the world.

My Tennis Pro Is Shot

In January, I wake up
with backhand anxiety.
I am fifteen, nearly
too old to change, and
winter is when I think
about the deadlines
for success, how others
meet them. With topspin.
With kick serves. I see
on an inside page
of the *Press,* a picture
of Stahovic, my foreign
pro, and learn he has
four bullets in him.
A column describes
his wounds, and I wonder,
at once, whether
conditioning will save him,
think of drugs and thieves
and outraged lovers,
list them like rankings:
I am #7 in Pittsburgh,
16 and under. No one
goes pro from there.

The Smokehouse

The union wrinkled and grayed
in a foreign tongue while
my family dreamed itself
backward to Germany —
scythe, sickle, the boot heel
across the face. For years,
their late, large voices
left English when they drank
in the clouded kitchens
of cheese and onions
and cured meat. Her winter
laundry on lines, the aunt
who said cold kept clothes
from spoiling showed me
the smokehouse where hams
dangled, where months of sausage
spun in our intruders' draft.
And after twenty years, after
I've shaken a funeral's worth
of hands and heard her brothers
rinse the room with anecdotes,
we follow the route where
the street's seams have split,
where tumors of weeds
have burst the asphalt
and the vandal boards
have been stripped from
the gouged eyes of storefronts.
The closed bars bunch men
like lockouts; there are thousands
of paper scraps clustered
at doorsteps, against curbs.
Some of them are speaking
when I wind down the window,
when I punch off the radio
and listen to translate
the neighborhood's riffle of wind.

Home Treatments

Boric acid, baking soda, the razor blade
Through the abscess — you could whimper, whine, and cry
Like a pantywaist, or take your medicine

Because you were putrid, because you sinned
And had to be reminded by physical signs
About what's in store for you, young man.

The evil was under my skin, in my bowels,
And home treatments worked as well as store-bought
To draw the poison out, to show me a sample

Of how things could worsen. Imagine the blade
Not cared for, the concentration raised like
A sucker's bet. I'd get something, then,

To cry about. I'd wish Lazarus could bring me
That hell-plea drop of water. I remembered
His home treatment, those street dogs that

Licked his sores. He wasn't that other
Lazarus raised from the dead, that doubled name
A hex, maybe, for everyone is equal,

For the pain that strengthened the spirit.
And what did I think: that failures could go
Untreated, that if I shut my eyes, they'd leave?

Throwing the Voice

> I know what to say by reading Bergen's lips.
> Charlie McCarthy

In Galesville, Wisconsin, if you follow
Signs selectively, you can discover
Where the Garden of Eden rose and fell,
Borders from which your parents were banished
According to Reverend D. O. VanSlyke,
Who thought God, if he'd had an ideal plan
For his fresh planet, would have started there.
The local color of pulpit logic:
In this Genesis, Noah, too, had come
To rest in Wisconsin, running aground
For man's second anachronistic chance,
And though those midwest mountains diminished
The Flood, VanSlyke had followers who liked
The idea of being pinpointed
On paradise, and one Sunday, while he
Accounted for the meaning in their lives,
My grandmother was born, so I'm writing,
This fall, during their dual centennials,
Imagining her, somehow, the VanSlyke
Chosen, a bright birth-sign exact upon
The American Eden. We all have
Our calendar twins, mine, I discovered,
The second sun day of Los Alamos,
And my grandmother insisted to me
That Pittsburgh, where we lived, was Edenic,
How the dark triangle of its rivers
Was the double dare Biblical symbol
Of paradise and sex. We stood downtown
Where the lax, late summer thighs met, and I
Listened to her parable voice saying:
"A man entered his furnace each evening
And crawled out unscathed, and he lived above
That fire until it choked on its ashes,

Went out, and slept him silent in its smoke."
We had sufficient hell in the steel mills,
She thought, to upgrade behavior; we had
Floods enough to make me believe, when they
Rose, we were only days from The Deluge.
I don't know what VanSlyke saw in his state
To make him select his provincial site,
But a beauty of fables lies upon
The planet like wood waiting to be voiced
By tongues tightened in the mouths of experts.
Look, we exclaim, the ventriloquist drinks
And the song of the dummy continues.

Oxygen

Somebody is always struggling with oxygen
Like Mrs. Oppenlander this summer, even
The memory of the word blocked as she recollects
Instead the boy I was when these tubes were elsewhere.
"How thin," visitors might say, "how precarious,"
As if adjectives were appropriate along
Highland Avenue, all the houses built before
The atomic scare, all of them turning to gray
Because they are older than I am — my clumsy
Logic, my noticing that the street-bed bricks are
The same pale ones I painted with watercolors
That August when lightning struck the steeple next door.

Thirty-seven, and I have returned to this street
Of lost breath where lung after lung fills like wineskins:
All of these stairs, all of these hot bedrooms carved out
Of tight attics that look out toward the dormant tracks.
How height deceives; how thirty years ago I stood
Upstairs and felt myself plunging to the sidewalk;
How we surprise ourselves and expect to mumble
"Where am I?" as the ordinary evening fills
With mucus, strangling after it lies down to sleep.

This could be the road where my children have listened
To their thin neighbor cough until he disappeared
The way Greismere Street climbs above my grandfather's
Sold and remodeled house, the first turn frightening
The flatlanders who visit, running the blind curve
Chance right onto the slick cobblestones, right along
The cliff's edge narrow lane where no one thought of cars
That could plummet into Etna like UFO's,
All shrieks and shattering glass — the mauve confusion,
The two-tiered Möbius strip of it carrying
Everybody back to his beginning, down from
The highest house where Fleischers, both unsteady from
The saw of surgery, watch the borough shrivel,
Talk of their new neighbors who erected a huge,

Brilliant cross at Christmas and drove off into
A holiday toll accident. "It's the thin air,"
They insist. "It's the leaning back into the slope
That disturbs balance and makes us gasp," and I add
A damp spring excuse for all of this breathless luck.

Thanksgiving

Some families, like mine, turn photographs
Toward the wall when relatives die, a kind
Of Last Man's Club, gathering the oldest
Generation together for flat bread
Before the young can reenter to feast
And shed their memories like heavy coats.
On Thanksgiving my parents set their smiles
For flashbulbs; we passed turkey and stuffing;
The children learned who faced away from them,
How the souls of the absent could listen.

Everyone at our table, at least once,
Must have considered screaming, running to
Those mounted faces to scan lips for breath
And speech. One year, for instance, with my aunts
And uncles thinning, I counted cousins
Who were close to me in age, careful as
A captain in one of those set-adrift
Lifeboat films, and I couldn't help guessing
The youngest would get to turn the last eyes
Of us to the wall because she had six
Years on me, three on her brother, and she
Didn't drink or smoke or have children of
Her own to hammer the valves of her heart.

I sat waiting for the business of loss
To close for another year and compared
Us to those old Tasmanians I'd read
About on the plane, a final couple
Left childless so there was nobody else
For the British to guard. They stuffed the husband.
They displayed him in a museum and waited
On the wife, not turning his face to the wall.
And Truganinny, the last Tasmanian
Woman, dreamed her husband's horror, dreamed her skin
Sewn shut over stuffing, dreamed the world's eyes
Stealing her stretched body forever. Maybe

There was a way to be secretly buried,
But Truganinny didn't find it. She made
The museum right there beside her husband,
Both of them in a permanent kind of pain,
And I showed those pictures to my children,
Asked them what those souls would murmur if they had
A Thanksgiving family to return to,
Though, at that altitude, with the clouds parted
And Pennsylvania brown beneath us, neither
Tried to guess what I wanted them to say.

The Developer's Landscape

The Developer's Landscape

Flash Flood

How does it feel at the end of science?
What's important the day after closure?
This flash flood drowned a priest, seven others,
So not even my mother is blaming
Original sin, and not one neighbor

Mistakes his house for Old Testament
Justice. Upstream, their alibi of clocks
Is ticking on the wrists of engineers,
But here, at street's end, Mrs. Cellendar
Tells me about the old woman who clung

To a light pole outside the butcher shop.
"Seventy-two," she says. "Imagine her
Lasting at my age." And surely, I can't,
But I nod while I stare into Pine Creek,
Focus on every wet day I walked here

After school, believing in dams. What do
We say when the heart of numbers shatters?
When the pulse of structures fibrillates, fails?
Mrs. Cellendar won't quiet; she keeps
Explaining, I think, because she's shrunk me

Inside her head to the boy she screamed at
For letting his father's trash fire settle
In her tree, a great puff of newspaper
Aflame in her wild cherry. "Yesterday,"
She says, "that pride of mine ran. It threw up

Its branches like a tie-walker who's heard
The train too late," and after I pivot
Again to mud, to water, to the tracks
That trust this channel south, she adds, "It was
Like each one of those swirling things turned human."

Watching the Onions

> In one experiment, an onion seemed to affect the growth of another nearby, unless glass was placed between them, blocking the influence of the onion's mitogenetic rays.
>
> News item, 1950

The doctors crept into the onion fields,
Crouched by the growing green shoots to listen,
To measure, to calculate what difference
In size might mean in onions. And they may
Have thought those plants the vegetable nightmare,
Something like The Thing thawing near our blood
In that year's alien invasion film.
Well, "Who Goes There?" it says in the credits,
Citing the source, and truly we should ask,
Or stand, as I did that May, behind my
Father's door, say "Nobody's home" to knocks
Or flat chimes. Because I wasn't challenged.
Because another ring, another rap,
And there was silence. My voice might have been
Full of mitogenetic rays. That spring,
In the windpipes of onions, there were soft
H's, the glottal fricatives of myth
That could rally stalks to giants. How we
Embellish our witness, how we employ
The adjectives of the mute, our fingers
As wands, as the way to magic. And if
It happens that one morning these rays are
Verified, we may recollect as well
The anesthesia soundtrack, what the nurse
Who whispered, "Count backwards from one hundred,"
Might have sung after ninety-eight, whether
She may have subtracted all the way to
Zero, whether the medicinal use
Of the imagined will walk us to farms
And lay us down near onions to be healed.

The Coronary Weight

In Pittsburgh, at Buhl Planetarium,
The pegs and pendulum clock whispered
The time, and each one of us who'd ridden
The school bus from Glenshaw bunched to wait for
Nine-fifteen to tumble. The near future
Was exactly on spot, stood two minutes
From the tap of physics, that quarter hour
Brushed, brushed, and nudged on schedule, the first lost
Bottle, that morning, of beer off the wall.
I figured forty-seven to follow,
A half day of Earth's story employing
The Poe prop, the sweep toward all of us bound
To the planet by the Inquisition.
And later, after we circled to watch
Blond Barbara Froelich's hair rise when she touched
The humming drum, I counted eleven
Stricken pegs and knew long-term residual
Effects were sparking in her foolish body —
Said the father in me, the grandfather,
The dead — which is how I'd aged from sitting
Under ceiling stars, having size defined
In so many universal ways I
Could hardly leave my seat. As if I were
On Jupiter, where I'd weigh, instead of
One hundred pounds, two hundred sixty-four,
According to the poster near the door.

The Titration Guess

Because, in the laboratory, opinion should be lost.

Because of thesis, test, observation, data.

Because what follows is retest, control group, conclusion,
and a season of scientific attack.

Because, in beginners' lab, I was sentenced to stand in front
of a cylinder calibrated in milliliters instead of ounce-fractions,
and everything in that room turned foreign as measurement
   language.

Because I could see, in my boredom, I was going to waste my
   future,
that every other student was releasing fluid into that cylinder
by drops: One, observe; two, observe; three, and still hours
of drops waiting to pearl and stretch and flop before anything
like change might happen.

Because I could have been feeding the blood of the early born,
watching for their eyes.

Because I opened my valve and let loose a stream that altered
nothing until, in my test solution, the rich red of dismay
ripened and rotted while, all over the lab, pale pink beakers
of success were blooming.

Because I subtracted two milliliters and entered the answer
in the workbook space I had to fill.

Because somewhere along the etched lines of my cylinder was
the perfect response, so why not the one I guessed?

Polywater

> First "discovered" in the Soviet Union, this "new"
> water was shown to be ordinary water with impurities
> by 1972, although papers documenting its existence
> continued to be published for several years.

In class, we took notes on the polywater lecture,
Were sent to the journals to secondhand research
What might end our world. The doomsday droplet
Might escape the lab. It might convert the water
We'd grown up with to poison, and I studied
Translations of the current Communist threat,
How the Russians were beating us to the punch
With liquid *Sputnik*. Somewhere in Leningrad
A professor like mine was measuring water.
He was singing a song I wouldn't be hearing
On the radio just before the broadcast was
Interrupted to tell us our rivers had turned

To syrup, the oceans were thick with success
Of science, and each locked ship had let down
Its sailors, like hair, into the mutant waves.

Faculty X

> The sense that sometimes comes to us of being present
> at past or distant scenes.
>   — Colin Wilson

One believer insists he's faced
The Führer, greeted Columbus
With a gift of beads, but history
Far off has caught the gist of me,
Turned featureless before I've
Verified identities. I might
As well be flipping the switch
In a late-night kitchen, trying
To recognize which vanishing
Roach has the face of Caesar
In the Pharisees' field guide
To the past. How we tally
These inventories of the vague.
How some of us speak our diaries,
Bring them to the Lourdes of
Microphones and cameras, waiting
For passages to heal: In college,
My job was to rearrange setups
In a psych lab. A professor
Had hired me to make sure table
And chairs and apparatus were
In place. Sometimes there were wires
And probes, sometimes just cards to
Choose from or the bare space of
Deprivation; and one evening,
As I finished shifting furniture
So some slow learner from
The local school could fumble

Circles and squares and triangles
Into a stew of anger, the girl
Who was with me slid her hands
Under my shirt to hurry me
Along. And when I reached for her
In return, I stared at the silver
Side of that wall-width mirror
No one used for dressing and lost
Myself in arrangements, thinking
Here a choice, there response,
Here reward or punishment,
And allowed myself the subject's
Trial and error sequence toward joy.

The High IQ of Nostalgia

The High IQ of Nostalgia

The hare, because it is born with open eyes, was
thought, by the Celts, to witness prenatal life.

One study cedes the earliest
Memories to the brightest.
At age three, at two, on the day
Of first steps, a sort of MENSA
For retrieval. Snow, I blurt,
The winter of '47.
Christmas, our fallen, blue-bulbed tree.
My mother's fur collar, the eyes
And noses of the sewn minks
Which formed it. My ringworm shave.
My steel-braced shoes. The neighbor
Who drowned in pneumonia.
On the Philco, "Tennessee Waltz,"
"Slow Boat to China." My father,
In the Chevy, singing "I've Got
A Lovely Bunch of Coconuts,"
Enough of each trip across
Pittsburgh retained to insure
The high IQ of nostalgia.

Nor need it end there, I've learned
From hypnotists who claim we can
Take the express trance back to birth,
Passing the whistle-stops for songs,
Weather, and trauma. Look. Listen.
Now concentrate. Now concentrate:
What was your mother's hairstyle?
— long, curled, held tight to the scalp
   with pastel, decorative pins.
What did the doctor murmur?
— it's warm. push, push. see, a boy,
   a big one, pink and heavy.
With what were you first handled?
— by the doctor's gloves, then forceps,
   tugging at the tardy head.

69

What did you see before birth?
— nothing. or else darkness. or else
   the landscape's been forgotten.

What about those months of absence,
The prenatal secrets erased
By oxytoxin's amnesia?
Opening our eyes to the lost
Prehistories, reschooling us
In the lanugo language?
Awakening again, prompted
By diminishment, we seek
The first motives for sucking
The thumb, for sipping the sea
In which we float, for closing
Our eyes against the sudden,
Outside light. And then, refusing
The stories spoken through the walls,
We backtrack, trusting our way
To the choice of the right hand,
The wiring up of the brain.
And, imploding, we retreat
Past unstoppable gender and
The great why of fertility,
Descending the reason list
Toward #1, all of us
Leaning backward to see and hear,
Paying attention, ready
To memorize whatever
Our trance-struck eyes insist is true.

Callback

This morning's rain is thorough:
Scranton, Harrisburg, part
of the news on each cable station.
So is our county's horse molester,
who's being covered out of town,
and I've watched the same dying mares
three times by eight-thirty, learning
the damage done by a baseball bat
with blades. Here are the farmers
closemouthed about wounds and rage
and cause; here are the horses
shrieking with violation, quivering
cross-state like the next atrocity
for the national news. I'm sitting
in front of these channels because
today my lungs are hysterical
with phlegm, breathing enormous,
walking or working postponed
while I wait for my prescription
to pay for itself. I have time
to see the next feature on Greenville,
another sick steel town north
of Pittsburgh. I've lived there.
I've graduated from the small college
that's shrunk, since then, like industry
and tax base. I've read poems there, too,
five years ago, so I don't need
this documentary to show me
how malignancy has spread. I took
my nostalgia walk; I paused,
late in March, at a window where
a Christmas tree lay sprawled inside,
and because it was artificial
and the store was abandoned,
I couldn't tell which year
it might have stood, how long ago

the owner had decorated knowing
his lease was lost, tossing tinsel
on those branches like a wig
over a chemotherapy skull.
The camera walks that street;
I cough and listen to every
steelworker say, "They'll be calling
us back, sooner or later," hackneyed
as our horse owners claiming,
"They'll catch the bastard soon,"
all of them poised like the shopkeeper
in this sequence who looks down
his sidewalk for business, waiting
for the first signs of restoration
that should come naturally as breath.

Commandments

Our neighbor had one kidney, two babies,
A doctor who said she'd murder herself
With the next one, and still she sat pregnant
Because the church had told her so. You can't
Say NO, can't slip anything in between
Yourself and the next soul waiting in line
To enter its earthly body. I knew
She'd taken the same marriage instructions
I had; she'd heard the homelife commandments
And maybe someone had stood up and said,
"Bless us, Father," like the man next to me
At my last session, five minutes before
I could leave and try to forget six hours
Over hell. So we all stood. We received
A blessing that inferred a curse on me
For seventeen items I'd heard, starting
With soiling myself and soiling others,
Including the woman by me who was
Going to wear the lace lie of white,
Curse herself with coils and pills to keep
Some souls in limbo jostling for a while.
And I'm thinking about how many times
I've changed my random places, fumbling for
The fortunate spot while my lines counted
Off by fours; drifted to the back each time
I had to climb the impossible ropes,
Leap into water to take swimming tests
That began where everyone said it was
Twenty feet down to the black lake's bottom.
"Just jump," one lifeguard muttered, and I did
Because there wasn't a NO. I couldn't
Refuse nearly drowning, swinging one arm
And then the other, slapping and splashing
And unable to cry for help as I
Swallowed warm lake water, went down, came up,
Went down and trusted the lifeguard or death

To explain the mystery. Look, the woman
Next door had her baby and didn't die
Either except for the divisible
Death dialysis brings, three times a week
Dragging her up from the toxic bottom.
I grabbed a doughnut balloon, let the man
On the boardwalk pull me in as if there
Were barbs stuck so far down my throat he'd yank
My guts out when he lifted me to flop
Along the pier. "It's a mystery to me,"
He said, "how someone can sink," and I knelt
To vomit, told myself NO, and didn't.

Nigger Island

> So named because of some unruly Negroes who had driven their owner away and had defied the authorities and were caught on this island.
> *Selinsgrove Times Tribune*

At noon, near the river, the guide
Untangles briars, bends sumac,
Tells us "Nigger Island's just north
Of the Isle of Que, a little
South of Shady Nook, and across
From Cherry Island." And though we
Ought to say Nat Turner, John Brown,
We listen to "There's a sinkhole
In the Susquehanna that's called
Nigger Deep," think ourselves police
Pulling oars, naming an island
With curses, wishing Nigger Deep
On those fugitives, the becalmed
Unruly who blended as best
They could into the brush, learning
The limits of camouflage, so
Vulnerable we can see them
Through our telescope of hindsight.

Their day drowned like the cramped, clutching
At light. This landmark sits so small
There's no hope of buried treasure
Mapped in cryptograms, and we stare
At our local slurs while this tour
Xeroxes the past, duplicates
The names for shame: Islands, sinkholes,
The push and pull of the landscape,
History we're hearing again, crossed
Out, erased, crumpled into balls
Like our doodles on the surface
Of this tour while our right response
Flounders breathless. Look, on both banks

Of this river we've stood watching
Police hooks trolling for bodies,
And still we've seen nothing return
From the water, no mannequins
Dragged into boats, no lost children
Lifting gasps from shore. Instead, we
Hear Nigger Island, Nigger Deep,
The hypnosis of names sending
Us upland to our painless homes.

Booths

In Ambridge, Pennsylvania, a host
Of people claim they've seen the eyes
Of Christ close on the crucifix
In a church, unison enough to
Drive me through this steel-slaughtered town

Where June after June I've visited
For a festival's main-street length
Of kielbasa, pierogies, and
Sweet potato pie sold from booths
By women from churches. Tourist,

White collar, I've lost the lust for sausage,
For anchovies that send out for beer,
But here where I park is someone, drunk,
Who might have swallowed thirty years
Of Armco steel, enough soot and smoke

To keep him thirsty for the rest
Of his laid-off life. "You're too late,"
He offers. "Jesus is over,"
And of course I smile and shrug and
Remember, suddenly, the cop

Who, outside the Garden Theater,
Said, "Sorry, you're too late, you missed it,"
Meaning *Deep Throat,* which had been raided
An hour before. My wife and I
Retreated, foolish with thinking

We'd missed one of those moments when
The eyelids of statues reopened,
Though there are booths now where anyone
Can stare at the sequels, where the film
Is looped so it's impossible

To be late. And some of those watchers
Open their throats at the glory holes
In those booths, do their Linda Lovelace
In spite of how AIDS might lay them off.
Christ, on Christmas Eve, driving in sleet

For presents, I found a rest stop
For my holiday season cramps
And faced four cars whose drivers were
Watching me like I was an oncoming,
Jackknifed truck. I walked into WOMEN.

I hooked the door of that dark stall
As if I were some giant dyke
Who wanted to be alone with herself.
I had needs. I listened for footsteps
And brainstormed the way the priest

Of this forlorn parish must have done,
Lost as Ambridge where the streetlights
Blink off early to save money;
Where, if anyone believed in
Secular hope, he'd claim he'd seen fire

At night, the riverbank spreading
To an open hearth to smelt all
Of the pointlessness left behind
When each of the steel mills closed.
So there might be the shrine that lasts,

A sort of lay Lourdes for employment.
Though I heard nothing but the men
Next door. Though the priest's traffic has
Turned to single cars, to gossip, regret;
And now I'm talking with someone

Who explains the priest is on retreat,
Resting and healing like steel, like
The hungover, like I thought I was
Healing in the car as I pulled
Back into the sleet imagining

The blowtorched dreams of night sweats,
The evening drowning of pneumonia,
The endgame splotches of sarcoma
That wake some men to flame, to ashes, to
The opening and closing of painted eyes.

Behind Glass

From the top tier of this resort hotel,
From behind the floor-to-ceiling glass
That buoys me like an enormous updraft,
I'm following the turns and plunges
Of a plane, how low it swoops to spray
Caterpillars who want these woods for food.
It veers so close I nearly flinch, silly
With reflex, though last week one pilot
Crashed, striking power lines half as high
As I'm standing with the first thought
Of toxins, how judgment might atrophy
In a daily mist of poison, how a pilot
Might think like a robin attacking glass,
Flying away and back until it fractures
Its neck on a rival's invisible cage.

Or perhaps I'm as safe as contestants
In the quiz show booths rolled out, one year,
When the swelling size of prizes made us
Believe that isolation mattered.
And what would we have said to Van Doren
Or Stempel (the whistle-blower) when
Jack Barry gave them time to think? And who
Could solve Shakespeare, spelling, opera or
Food for sixty-four thousand dollars?
"Do you want to continue?" Hal March asked,
And a few people stopped, believing
Eight thousand dollars wonder enough,
Leaving the glass booth before the answers
Entered their ears like annunciation.

Now, in film clips, when those careful,
Coached geniuses pretend to ponder
Inside that glass, they seem as alien
As a waving pope or his would-be killer
In court. As Eichmann. As the Mafia
Kingpins from Sicily, listening,

We think, to the unedited language
Of their public trials. None of those
Boxed gangsters expected the Stempel
Of crime lords to confess and convict.
None of them needed a prompter to lead
Them to the championship of denial.

And what of those B-film space helmets,
The fishbowls the commanders removed
Like white lab rats on remote planets?
They'd inhale once and tell their nervous crews
"It's OK to breathe," though there was no sign
Of plants, nothing but rocks and the rubber
Monsters which flourished on every new world.
And we knew what happened when the captains
Didn't chance the air: One helmet was flawed.
Some spaceman would clutch, suddenly, his glass,
And we'd see his mouth working for answers.

The A Capella Rehab

The harmonies of morning
Chuff softly from the highway—
Shift and brake, acceleration,
Occasional horn. I'm up
So early with exercise
I stretch without old music,
My doo-wop and a capella
Records in the dark while I work
The diminished sculpture
Of my knee to resurrect sprint
And squat, the pivot and push off
Of the past. Facedown in carpet,
I slip one hand's noose around
An ankle, apply the dreaded
Step-over toehold of rehab
Like a villain wrestler.
The Executioner, I think.
The Crusher. Some masked threat
Faking this therapy for trauma,
Though lately I've let myself
Be pinned for the X ray, played
Dead for the soft-tissue test
Of the MRI, locking my knee
Through the jackhammer of scan
And sketch. I've sung the litany
Of ligaments, cartilage,
Tendons, bone. I've hummed
The ceiling-speaker Muzak while
Blue conduction-gel readied me
For ultrasound's problematic
Healing. I've grunted foot-pounds
Of force into jagged peaks
On a calibrated screen:
Lift and resist. Extend and pull
To bring back the reconstructed
Harmony of the knee, decades

Draining like fluid until
Old voices might impossibly
Gather: The Students. The Schoolboys.
The Teenchords — all those group names
For transience repeated
Like a mantra of nostalgia:
To silence the strange beetle's click
Of walking. To validate how
Beer and music might stabilize
A knee. To prove how palm oil,
Butterfat, and egg yolk might coat
The tongue of the lizard of pain.
To announce, between punishments,
The Gestapo Actuary will
Wrestle all comers, replacing
Johnny Valentine's backbreaker
And the enormous body drop
Of Haystacks Calhoun with
The submission hold of statistics.

Working the Eighteen-Inch Seam

"It's not done," Jerry Bell says,
and his father finishes the beer
I've bought him before he says
"Yes" and uses his expression
to tell me nobody talks about
the slithering face-first
into dust. It's like the war;
it's like a disease chewing
you up but not forcing a word
out of your Mafia mouth,
and I admit it's my father's way,
my uncle's, everybody born
seventy years ago to labor
as if they made a pact to suffer
as mutes. Jerry Bell wanted
to tell me anything worth
hearing about the mines;
I wanted to spill my stories
about the mills, and both of us
nodded and waved empty glasses
toward a woman who had never
heard of her husband's pain.

U-turn

Just once I've braked the car,
squealed a U-turn that sprayed
gravel and pointed us back
to where we'd started. My sons
asked when I'd turn again, keep
vacation in front of us,
but I was concentrating on
not tumbling off the sudden,
steep pitch of the highway.

One by one they stopped whining
and vanished. My wife stared
and stared and her seat emptied,
leaving me in 1965, at least,
the last time I didn't have
someone talking to me.
Now I could believe I'd never
graduate from anywhere;
I'd never drive into Pittsburgh
to shove family-size cans
into steam whose pressure
I'd trust to an Italian
who drank whiskey for lunch.

It's 1965 if I see Linda Hanzel
giving me directions to forget her,
if Cathi with an *i* sends a friend
to her door to tell me she's bored.
I'm punching in at 6:45
every Monday through Friday,
and when I've cashed the union's rate,
I'm driving my father's car
with the needle buried under ninety
until one evening I read a name
I know inside a wreckage story.

Except for the deaths that
were starting, the days were copies.

I was singing "It ain't me, babe"
like Dylan because I needed,
for once, an excuse to leave
a girl, steering straight ahead,
missing all the strangers
who've stood too far into the road
to be just looking at the sky,
trusting me to be reading
the traffic for the single break
where my swerve would be harmless
as a U-turn shouting nothing
but "you are" or "you believe."

The Hot Wings Wager

A dozen wings that triggered tears,
Revved the wheeze and cough of reflex
With jalapeño and japones,
Guero and tepin, mulato and
The chiles unnamed and mythical
As holy mushrooms. I was ready
To spend my winnings on beer and shrimp,
Authentic blues in an uptown bar.
"Hot cherry," I said, "cayenne," reciting
My picante vita, claiming ten minutes
Of pain so tiny I'd laugh, later,
At apprehension. And I thought
Of my father, who believes in
The green pepper, and the green pepper
Only. Who swears food on the table
Shows a man for who he is, and wishes,
Therefore, for the selfish to choke,
The rich to aspirate and hurry
Themselves to hell. Like this, I thought,
Swallowing fire like a flame eater,
Bolting four, frantic to finish,
And recognizing, more clearly
Than ever, the scald of stupid choice.
Five. Six. "Halfway to paradise,"
The cook explained — something like sex,
Like the multiplications of faith.
Seven and stalled. Eight and the betrayal
Of the esophagus and stomach,
The giveback of foolishness to
The visible world. Though even
After vomit, after the violence
Of the body's refusal, I was
Regretting its checks and balances,
How we're limited by the sober
Sonata of involuntary sense.

The Snowball Protest

My son said he stood in snow
To shout he hated college
And the cops. Someone he knew
Had broken forty windows
With a curved-blade hockey stick,
Circumnavigating the dorm,
Returning like the sailor
Who brought home Magellan's ship.

I said it seemed the Sixties,
Window after window touched
Like destruction's rosary.
He told me the cops hated
The hard-packed slush of March, that
He'd bruised one Gestapo face,
At least, in the snowball protest,
Before everybody ran,
Before the troopers whacked him
Against the bricks, pummeling with
Pussy, asshole, fuck you and
Your friends while they cuffed his wrists.

Disorderly conduct, public
Nuisance, accessory to
Mayhem. In the nightstick
Evening, he was learning something
From the spontaneous syntax
Of anger: The humiliation
Of bondage. The powerlessness
Of reason. How his words would
Not pack in the near zero
Of interrogation. How they
Sprayed into lace that blew back
In his eyes before they blinked.

The Thoreau Cane

We hear the story of the man
Who shot his wife for too often
Serving beans. "Wouldn't you be mad?"
He said, as if all of us might
Form lines to shoot, remembering
Carrots and oatmeal, liver and
A list of avoidable hates.
We learn the tale of the teacher
Who rewarded her good students
By having them spit on the bad.
And once, in Pittsburgh, a banker
Spanked customers late with their loan
Repayments, teaching his lessons
Like the sergeant who built human
Xylophones from his new recruits,
Each of them with a note to sing
When he was pummeled with a bat.

And Thoreau's cane? One afternoon
He lifted it, flogged six students,
Each of them chosen at random
To show his principal he could
Punish, one way of responding
To the leniency reprimand
Before resigning and walking
Out on the expectation of
Regular canings in Concord.

So often, so consistently
In this anguish curriculum,
The punishers are jittery
With certainties: The Dreyfus "D";
The Mudd splint; the packed, Scottsboro
Boxcar. We speak of Leo Frank,
Lynched by the Gentile mob; outside
It's August, the maintenance crew
Dragging desks, balancing a set

Of shelves, and hoisting the boxes
Full of books in weather so warm
The air seems furred, capable of
Spontaneous combustion like
Handpicked sinners disappearing
In sudden flames. For crimes, we're told,
In the punishment seminar,
In these texts for hidden loathings.

The Asthma Revenge

> I'm not going to make it this time.
>
> Richard Green

1

"Get back, give him air," somebody
Always shouts, meaning oxygen,
Great gulps from those plastic cups
At the faces of spent athletes.
Yet lately I've been reading
That oxygen burns us, heats this
Page yellow to brown to ashes.
The theatrical air ignites;
Each atom strikes and sears our words.

2

The degree was Richard Green's:
Doctor of Laws, Honoris Causa.
The biographical sketch was read,
And we listened, at graduation,
To why and why not he was there.
The sun was fixed, behind the stage,
At eye level. The President was
A silhouette; the dead Chancellor's Aide
Was a silhouette; and we extended
Our applause as if it might conjure
A curtain call. Suddenly, the failed
Encore entered my chest, some shallow
Empathy for the dead. I whistled
The Richard Green chorus; the gowns
Of the graduates turned into earth.

3

In public buildings, in the asbestos
Inside our walls. In the petri dish where

Something soft with filaments is blooming
To preview what will flower in our lungs.
In the smoke laws layered like cheap paint, rule
Over rule for sad public air. In how
We see the deep sunsets of their failure.
In headaches, nausea, persistent malaise.
In carbon, sulfur; bacteria counts
That can alter the blood's old color.
In learning, this morning, reprieve's cheap joy,
Passing grades on the PFT breath tube.
In hurrying with steady breath, relaxed,
Today, far from the sure saw and suture.
In the blood's future, in temporary help
That peels the false ceiling of my workplace,
Tears everything to flaking chunks. In me,
My stopped breathing while the men grab and rip,
Inhale and don't mention one thing aloud
About whether or not they might worry.
In slaving, once, with a summer work crew
That tore out ten rooms of insulation.
In all of us bringing beer to wash down
That dry snow. In laughing during our breaks
At black-lung jokes. In shifting the old wit
Of leprosy, polio, birth defects.
In how we need this work, prying out
The mistakes of our past, risking ourselves
And not admitting we love the danger
And expect to stay untouched, our children
Kept from poison even as the cough starts
In sleep at rising so we can chuckle
That we clear our systems like the engines
Of our morning cars. In the way we are
Miners in the air. In how we're propping
Passages behind us, feeling our way
Through an atmosphere suffering with seams.
In the early scrub of the sky, such streaks
We might whisper how careless this cleaning.

4

On the last afternoon of her life my mother wrote and mailed her
weekly news to me. After the funeral, after travel, my neighbor
passed me her note. That letter lay warm in my hands; it yellowed
and curled from the air I was drawing toward me and the language
on the page, the signature in flames, the return address affixed in
the envelope's corner as it's supposed to be, insurance against loss.

5

Traveling, I snapped
my glasses, the frames
falling in near halves
to the motel carpet.
The floor faded and
flew down. Its cables
had snapped; the room's air
followed, and I might
have been the first tenant,
the one who haunts
the nightly renters.
They dream of smoke,
wake to a stranger
who's replaced the air
with his foggy voice.

6

When asthma returns,
I check back for sins,
Some, at least, enough
To stifle breathing.
In each lung cell is
My mother, telling
Me about vengeance
And God's awful fire.
I wheeze under stress;
My sons wheeze in wind;
Someone is paying
Me back and singing

The Richard Green song;
Someone is paying
Me back and there are
Hours when the lost
Pittsburgh mills shoot soot
Through my lungs from
Their foreign steel graves.
The Old Testament
Lives here; it's lasted
Ten banked-furnace years.
So Western Culture
Absorbs us, birched by
The old lessons; so
Shame is better shared,
And each airless dream
Of death that wakes me
To inhalator
And regret, says real
Death is for others
Who wake up drowning
In their sea-dark rooms.

7

The fingerprints of our breathing collect
On the CFC panes of our skies, and
We see where the clear ceiling has formed.
The confusion of air: we think, standing
At our open windows in disbelief,
That surely we'll resurface, untangle
Ourselves from the knots of our house-lake's floor.
The windows in this room face south, double
Paned and large to warm our house in winter.
Beside me, a dozen plants are arranged
Like a yearbook photo. I'm looking at
The tallest, reaching to this riser's rear
As if this touching releases the air
From leaves. This is how we burn more quickly,
Refuting the maxim: all over our
Lives, the assault of the defiant air.

In the Census Year

Last night, because my daughter talked too long
Through too many rooms, I kicked the cordless phone,
Chased its scuttling legs across the floor to stomp
The numbered face for each of the Furies
Pursuing me, gutting it at five, laying it
Open at seven, and throwing it, finally,
Against the piano she hadn't touched since
She was nine. It bounced through my frenzy
Like a resilient martyr. It splayed
Into icon on the carpet, and I cursed
Those numbers one through zero, damned
The area code and redial, and wished Job's hands
On the throat of God. I wanted the world's
Full list of victims armed and besieging
Whichever paradise enslaves them, and when
It was certain no miracle was re-forming
That phone, I opened its book and recited
Abers, William 743–0017;
Abrahaims, Edward 743–2103;
The start of one more fraudulent penance
For the stupid sins of the damaged brain.

I'd been reading how Patient "K" could quote
The Atlas, reciting the numbers for
Each U.S. town grown over 5,000.
He'd answered Sayre, Scottdale, and Sharon Hill
When tested near the minimum line, and
If he were questioned now, he'd offer
Selinsgrove — 5,227, naming
Where I stand shaking my rube's head
At these carnival claims, suspicious
Of the alligator boys and ape women,
Rigged-wheel promises like this census form
In the mail, the long version that scratches
My scabs for numbers, for explication.

I think of lying, claiming one more child,
Aunts in the spare room, an uncle upstairs,

A cousin who can total recall the weather
For each day of his life: The relative
Humidity of every August 10th.
The seven mornings plunged twenty below.
The thirteen days with snow lightning.
And while he repeats sleet, whiteout, hail,
I could listen for the singular days
Since October 12, 1955, when, three years
And seven months old, all of his flashbacks end
At rain beginning in the afternoon, turning
Colder, the clouds preventing overnight frost.
And always, at the loop's conclusion, so much
Silence before that mid-fall noon, it could
Have been creation, the weather as void,
Nothing in a newspaper to convince him
The day before had sun and clouds, sixty degrees,
That someone recorded such things to save them.

The Hollow Earth

I'm working a book of claims where records
Warm zero's boredom, where chapters debate
The first man to the pole, testing the tales
Of Peary, Cook, Byrd, and Schmidt, so many
Pages of lament for disputed truth,
So much grief for returning from ice.
From war, I add; from belief, sitting on
A wall built to keep the Susquehanna
From occasionally killing. I love
The lines near its top: the first place crest
Of Agnes, the record for this decade,
The one to commemorate "thirty-six."
Behind me, there's an "Agnes if" red stripe
Near the roof of a house, and I'm reading
That photographs from space have shown shadows
Near the poles, entrances, if you believe
The Hollow Earth Society, to huge
Holes to heaven missed by every pole dash.
Someone named Symmes made a map, asked Congress
To fund him north. He wanted to carry
Our flag down the tunnel, claim Inner Earth
For the U.S.; and Hitler, I learn next,
Believed in Symmes, stuck in a submarine
Under the South Pole ice according to
One more high-water marker of the crazed.
He's directing this year's atrocities;
He's governing the South Hole while his sins
Rise like propellants, thinning the ozone.
Look, Tarzan found his way inside. He walked
Into Pellucidar before Hitler
Arrived to organize those cavemen, strap
Weapons to those dinosaurs and turn one
More children's book to allegory like
Any secret place where we dream ourselves
Dark with death that cannot touch us. We dig
Our holes to China; we enter gold mines;

We lower ourselves into caves and work
The black labyrinth to the inside world.
Great Expectations, Columbine Crawl — now,
In Wyoming, there are cavers reaching
Records for depth, sliding against the snatch
Of Velcro rock, slithering through a crack
Called The Grim Crawl of Death, willing to creep
One more cruel corridor to paradise.
Passage to India, Northwest Passage —
All of these myths we long for from inside
The ghost-land of our basements, of wide pipes
We can walk the water with, expecting
The road to Shamballah or an entrance
Guarded by a flaming sword, plunging toward
That land lit always by a central sun.